REX

Collections

LED ZEPPELIN

Collections

LED ZEPPELIN

RAY TEDMAN

Reynolds & Hearn Ltd
London

ACKNOWLEDGEMENTS

When trying to tell the complex story of Led Zeppelin there are a multiplicity of sources.
I am particularly indebted to Stephen Davis's 'Hammer of the Gods', 'Led Zeppelin – a
celebration' by Dave Lewis, 'Led Zeppelin 1968-1980 – the story of a band and their music'
by Keith Shadwick and 'Led Zeppelin – the concert file' by Dave Lewis and Simon Pallett.
I am also grateful for Dave Lewis's help in dating some of the photographs. Dave's website
www.tightbutloose.co.uk is a must for Zepp fans. The mistakes are my own.

Ray Tedman, Spain, September 2007

This edition published in 2008 by
Reynolds & Hearn Ltd
61a Priory Road
Kew Gardens
Richmond
Surrey TW9 3DH

Images © Rex Features 2008
Text © Ray Tedman 2008

A CIP catalogue record for this book is available from the British Library.

ISBN (hardback) 978 1 905287 52 9   ISBN (paperback) 978 1 905287 86 4

Designed by James King

Printed and bound by Replika Press Pvt Ltd, Kundli, Sonepat (Haryana), India

CONTENTS

1. FOUNDATIONS

In the quiet churchyard of St Michael's, Rushock, in the English Midlands county of Worcestershire an unremarkable gravestone reads:

> Cherished memories of a
> loving husband and father
> John Henry Bonham who
> died Sept 25th 1980 aged
> 32 years. He will always be
> remembered in our hearts.
> Goodnight my love,
> God bless.

Unremarkable, that is, except for the mass of drum sticks, CD cases and other memorabilia placed against the headstone, for this is the last resting place of John 'Bonzo' Bonham, drummer of Led Zeppelin. Bonham's tragic death marked the end of a group that had dominated rock from the release of its first album *Led Zeppelin* in 1969.

From the end to the beginning. It all started with Jimmy Page. Born in 1944, Jimmy lived a comfortable, if solitary life as the only child of middle-class parents. At the age of 15 he acquired his first acoustic guitar, quickly graduating to a British-made copy of the Fender Stratocaster. By 1961 Jimmy was playing in a pro band, Neil Christian and the Crusaders, performing Chuck Berry and Bo Diddley covers. The strain of touring was too much for the young Jimmy and he left the band to enrol in art school.

Meanwhile, the British blues craze was gathering pace. Alexis Korner and Cyril Davies formed the band Blues Incorporated which, by 1962, included Mick Jagger, Charlie Watts and Jack Bruce in the line up. Mick and Charlie soon left to form the Rolling Stones but Blues Incorporated continued to pack them in at the Marquee in London's Oxford Street. It wasn't long before Jimmy picked up his guitar again, gaining confidence by jamming with Cyril Davies' interval band at the marquee, where, among others, he was complimented on his playing by Eric Clapton, then playing lead guitar with the Yardbirds.

In spite of receiving offers to become lead guitarist in several of the new bands springing up in the wake of the Beatles and Rolling Stones, Jimmy decided to work as a session guitarist. 'Little' Jim Page was much in demand as a studio musician working with such luminaries as The Who, The Kinks, Them and Van Morrison. Jimmy also dipped his toe into production, soon being hired by Andrew Oldham (the Stones' manager) as a staff producer for Oldham's Immediate Records. Here he worked with a wide range of artists, well-known and unknown, among them Chris Farlowe, Nico and John Mayall's Bluesbreakers (with lead guitarist Eric Clapton, who had left the Yardbirds after an argument about the release of a non-blues single (and worldwide hit) by the group). Jimmy had been invited to join the Yardbirds at that time but, to avoid offending Eric, Jimmy recommended they take on Jeff Beck instead.

By 1966 Jimmy was finding the lucrative work of session musician and producer a drudge. To add variety he was experimenting with his technique. A session violinist suggested Jimmy tried bowing his guitar. Jimmy had a go and was excited by the wild distorted sounds coming from the speakers. Thus a trademark was born. In spring of the same year came a second invitation. In spite of the tensions Jimmy saw in the Yardbirds (including a disastrous performance at an Oxford University May Ball) he joined the band, playing bass in the first instance at a gig at the Marquee in June 1966.

The Yardbirds left for an American tour in August, Jimmy still playing bass. The group were due to play the Carousel Ballroom in San Francisco when Jeff Beck refused to perform because of a sore throat. The fans' disappointment at the non-appearance of Beck was assuaged by a dazzling performance by Jimmy on lead guitar, complete with bowing sequences.

The tour completed, the band was re-organized with Jimmy and Jeff on lead guitars and Chris Dreja on bass. After shooting a sequence in England for Antonioni's film *Blowup*, the band left for a further tour of America in October. Shortly after the beginning of the tour, Beck quit the band. Although Beck asked to return a few days later, the three original Yardbirds refused.

The quartet continued, with Jimmy pushing the boundaries of his technique with the use of the bow and skilled use of a wah-wah pedal. However, the days of the Yardbirds were numbered. Disputes with their record company and drug-related problems meant that, by 1967, the downward slide had begun. Such singles as were released flopped. The band spent the latter part of 1967 touring the States with their new manager Peter Grant, but there was to be no revival. The members were split over the band's direction, with Page wanting to play the kind of music that Led Zeppelin would become world famous for. The glamorous venue of Luton Technical College in Bedfordshire saw the band's last performance on 7 July 1968.

Jimmy and manager Peter Grant saw the demise of the Yardbirds as an opportunity to create a group which could tap into the US market for 'heavy' music, where groups like Iron Butterfly and Vanilla Fudge had been fantastically successful. Jimmy had seen the problems bad management had caused the Yardbirds and was determined never to be in that situation again. He and Grant set up a new company which freed them from the Yardbird mess, and which meant that the new band would be self-owned and financially and artistically independent.

To honour the contractual obligation for a Yardbird tour of Scandinavia, there had to be a band. First stop: find a vocalist. Jimmy wanted a singer called Terry Reid but he had been snapped up by Mickie Most. Reid suggested a Birmingham singer, a tall blonde shouter billed as 'The wild man of blues from the Black Country'. His name was Robert Plant. After hearing Plant perform and inviting him to his base in Pangbourne, Jimmy was convinced he had found his vocalist. Now he needed a drummer. Plant came up with a name: John Bonham. Bonham, from Redditch, had been around the same music scene as Robert and was now playing with Tim Rose for the princely sum of £40.00 a week. Bonzo (as John Bonham was known) was reluctant to leave a secure seat for the New Yardbirds but was eventually persuaded by Plant and Grant, in the face of other offers from Chris Farlowe and Joe Cocker.

However, the jigsaw was not complete. Chris Dreja, former Yardbirds bass player, was originally slated for the new group, but at a late stage he decided to pursue his interest in photography. John Paul Jones (real name John Baldwin), a successful session bass player and producer had heard that Jimmy was starting a new group. 'Call me if you need a bass player'. Jimmy made the call.

On 14 September 1968 the New Yardbirds left for Denmark. The Scandinavian tour was the crucible in which the group's magic was created, particularly the sound of Plant's voice with Jimmy's guitar at full belt. Also out of the tour came a new name. No longer the New Yardbirds but Lead Zeppelin: The Who's John Entwhistle's term for a bad gig ('going down like a lead zeppelin'). Lead was changed to Led in short order to avoid Americans pronouncing it 'leed'.

The unique jigsaw was complete.

The Yardbirds 1964: (left to right)
Jim McCarthy, Paul Samwell-Smith,
Eric Clapton, Chris Dreja, Keith Relf

The Yardbirds 1966 with Jeff Beck
and Jimmy Page (front left and right)

2. TAKE-OFF

In October the band were in Olympic Studios in Barnes, South London recording *Led Zeppelin.* In 36 hours of studio time they laid down the nine tracks, at a cost, Peter Grant later claimed, of £1750.00, including the cover artwork of the fiery end of the zeppelin *Hindenburg.*

Once the studio sessions were completed, Grant attempted get some bookings for a quick English tour. The only problem was that no one wanted to book the New Yardbirds (old history) or Led Zeppelin (Who?). Jimmy told Grant to take any booking, whatever the billing and whatever the deal. The result was that Led Zeppelin made their debut at Surrey University, sharing a fee of £150.00, following this with a gig at the Marquee in London as 'Jimmy Page with the New Yardbirds' and a final appearance as the New Yardbirds at Liverpool University. The short tour over, the transformation was complete. The New Yardbirds were dead, long live Led Zeppelin!

The band had a strong line-up, a musical style, and a name. Now they needed a deal. In November 1968 Peter Grant flew to New York clutching the rough mix tape and sleeve artwork for *Led Zeppelin* to get a world distribution contract with an American record company without giving away the group's artistic and commercial independence. Grant had already held telephone conversations with Jerry Wexler of Atlantic Records, who made it clear that Atlantic wanted to sign Led Zeppelin. Amongst others, Wexler had had a glowing report of the group from Dusty Springfield.

Wexler, and Ahmet Ertegun (co-founder of Atlantic Records) saw Led Zeppelin as natural successors to the market stimulated by Iron Butterfly, Vanilla Fudge and, latterly Eric Clapton. Grant was knocking at an open door and was able to call Jimmy to tell him that he had negotiated a dream deal. Led Zeppelin would appear on the Atlantic label (the first white rock band to do so). Atlantic would distribute the records worldwide while leaving complete artistic control in the band's hands. For this agreement Led Zeppelin would receive an advance of $200,000 and the highest royalty rate ever agreed for a group of musicians. Jimmy arrived in New York a few days later to sign the agreement, bringing with him the master tapes for *Led Zeppelin.*

Back in the UK in December it was a very different picture. The band was still struggling to get bookings. In the run-up to Christmas they had a gig at the Marquee, played Bath Pavilion for £75.00, Exeter City Hall for £125.00, and ended their short tour in the salubrious surroundings of Fishmongers Hall, Wood Green, London. The scene was so grim that Jimmy and Peter decided to open their American tour early despite the fact that the album had not yet been released. On Christmas day 1968, the Zepps left London for Los Angeles.

In Los Angeles the group hooked up with their new road manager Richard Cole and headed for their first US date in Denver. Then it was off to the east coast to play the Tea Party in Boston. With an audience drawn largely from the huge college population, the gig extended from the original hour to an hour-and-a-half and then to seven encores. After a brief visit to New York it was back to the west coast, and after various adventures in snowbound Portland, Oregon to successful shows at the Whiskey in Los Angeles and the Fillmore West in San Francisco.

Led Zeppelin was released in the US in the last week in January (although some radio stations had been playing tracks from the album for weeks). Album sales were strong and there was plenty of airplay. *Rolling Stone* rather spoilt the party with a highly critical review. Zeppelin's reply was a stunning performance at New York's Fillmore East - a fantastic end to their first US tour.

The line-up 1969 (left to right) John Bonham, Robert Plant, John Paul Jones, Jimmy Page

Led Zeppelin at the Chateau Marmont
Hotel, Hollywood, during their second
1969 US tour

1

CITY OF THE ANGELS

3.

After the triumph of the first American tour, the return to the UK in February 1969 brought the band down with a bump. They were back to playing the clubs around London, often with an audience of around 400. For variety there was a short tour of Denmark and Sweden and a first (and only) live performance on BBC television. The UK release of *Led Zeppelin* at the end of March was largely ignored at the time. Disenchanted with the scene at home, Led Zeppelin returned to Los Angeles on 20 April for another tour, again in the tender care of road manager Richard Cole. They made their base in the Chateau Marmont hotel, where bungalows allowed privacy for the group to enjoy the rock 'n' roll lifestyle. The first stop on the tour was a four-nighter at the Fillmore West in San Francisco. The set was getting longer and longer, stretching an hour into a mind-blowing three-and-a-half hour assault on the senses.

In early May *Led Zeppelin* was in the US Top Ten. Onstage the band was on fire, offstage there was an endless supply of inebriating substances and attractive young women who were keen to be part of the Zeppelin experience. The band moved from Seattle to British Columbia, to Detroit (via a couple of days R&R in Hawaii) in a haze of alcohol and heavy partying. Journalist Ellen Sander who was on assignment from *Life* magazine covering the tour wrote 'No matter how miserably the group failed to keep their behaviour up to a basic human level... they played well almost every night of the tour.' The tour ground on. Athens, Ohio, Minneapolis, Chicago, Maryland, Boston and finally two nights at Fillmore East, New York on 30 and 31 May. Ellen Sander's view of the tour was bitter 'If you walk inside the cages at the zoo you get to see the animals close up, stroke the captive pelts, and mingle with the energy behind the mystique. You also get to smell the shit firsthand.'

In June the band were back in the UK, starting a home tour. Finally they were being recognised in their own country. They played three times on the BBC, including an hour's live show, followed by a set at the Bath Festival of Blues and a headlining slot at the Pop Proms at the Albert Hall. Although success was building at home, Led Zeppelin left for the US in July for another tour with over 20 appearances ending in August at the Texas International Festival. After a short break in September the band were back on the road with dates in Paris and London followed by the opening of another US tour at New York's Carnegie Hall.

While touring, the band had been working on their next album, *Led Zeppelin II.* It was released in the US on 31 October, with advance orders totalling 500,000. Entering the chart at 15, it reached number one by December 1969, displacing the Beatles' *Abbey Road.* By April 1970, US sales totalled three million. In the UK the album, released on 8 November 1969, got to number one in February 1970, occupying a place in the chart for a total of 138 weeks. In the US the track that got the most airplay was 'Whole Lotta Love'. But at five-and-a-half -minutes, the track was too long for many stations. Without permission, many stations simply edited out the middle section. Against the band's wishes, Atlantic released a single with the slimmed-down version which sold a million copies. Jimmy was furious. 'I just don't like releasing album tracks as singles. The two fields are not related scenes in my mind.'

At the beginning of November the band played the final concert of their tour at Winterland in San Francisco, in front of a worshipping audience. Led Zeppelin had been touring for nine months of 1969 and they returned home to recharge their batteries, spend time with their families and enjoy the benfits of the money they had earned.

Group photo, 1969

MORE POPULAR
4. THAN THE BEATLES

Refreshed, the band began 1970 with a seven date tour of the England, this time with no support acts. Starting in Birmingham and including a gig at the Albert Hall, the band added a new layer of sound with bass-player John Paul Jones playing Hammond organ. It became clear that Led Zeppelin were more than able to sustain a concert alone.

Following Robert Plant's minor injuries when he crashed his Jaguar early in February, the Zepps left for their first European tour on 21 February. The trip was enlivened when the band, threatened with legal action for use of the Zeppelin name by a descendant of Count von Zeppelin, appeared in Copenhagen as 'The Nobs'. Further excitement came when John Bonham and road manager Richard Cole got into a fight with two journalists at a press reception held in a Copenhagen art gallery.

The European tour ended on 13 March at the Montreux Jazz Festival. After a short break, the band launched in to their fifth North American tour, starting with a concert in Vancouver on 21 March. The Canadian leg of the tour went (in Zepp terms) calmly. Peter Grant mistook a Canadian government official checking sound levels for a bootlegger and smashed his equipment while (at the same concert) Bonzo trashed his dressing room.

The US part of the tour was something else. The Vietnam war had split American society, with the majority of college-age citizens opposing the war, and hostile to the government and its agencies who, in turn, saw anti-war activities as unpatriotic and a threat to legitimate authority. Led Zeppelin, so closely identified with rebellious youth, were clearly part of the problem. The police were out in force at many of the gigs, and clashes between the fans and the police forced the band off stage more than once. When the tour headed south there were more problems. In Memphis the four Zepps were, like Carl Perkins and Elvis Presley, made honorary citizens. This honour notwithstanding, such was the hostility of

certain sections of the American population that the group had to hire private security to protect them from, amongst others, an often hostile police force. On 19 April the exhausted Zepps closed their tour in Phoenix, Arizona, having played a total of 29 concerts.

Back in England the band took a well-earned break. At the same time they knew that a new album was expected by their record company. In May Robert suggested to Jimmy that they retreat to a small cottage in central Wales called Bron yr Aur (hill of gold). Thus it was that the pair, Robert's wife Maureen and 18 month-old daughter Carmen, Jimmy's girlfriend Charlotte Martin and three roadies spent a bucolic time while many of the tracks for *Led Zeppelin III* took shape. Recording for the new album took place Headley Grange, Hampshire and London's Olympic Studios, and was completed by the middle of June.

It was time to go back on the road. After warm-up gigs in Iceland, the Zepps played the Bath Festival. An audience of 150,000 had gathered to hear, among others, the Byrds, Jefferson Airplane, Santana - and Led Zeppelin. Playing against a spectacular sunset, the group finally established their superstar status in their own country.

Following a short three-gig trip to Germany, US tour number six began on 5 August in Cincinnati, Ohio. Each concert was undiluted Zeppelin, no support, no set, just amps, lights and blinding performances. While the band performed in Hawaii, back in the UK *Melody Maker* announced that Led Zeppelin had toppled the Beatles to become Top Group in their annual readers' poll.

This silver lining at the end of a hectic year had its cloud. *Led Zeppelin III* was released on 5 October in the US to luke-warm enthusiasm from the fans and hostility from the press. In a further twist, on 16 October the group were presented with gold discs by a government minister who recognised their 'Substantial contributions to the country's healthy balance of exports.'

Robert and Maureen Plant, 1970

Bonzo, Robert and John Paul Jones with Sandy
Denny (who joined the group on 'The Ballad of
Evermore' on *Led Zeppelin IV*)

Bath Festival of Blues, 28 June 1970

Albert Hall concert, 9 January 1970

SIGNS AND SYMBOLS

5.

The cool reaction to *Led Zeppelin III* was a catalyst. Jimmy and Robert retreated to Bron-yr-Aur to work intensively on new material. In December 1970 the group assembled at Island Studios to begin work on the next album. Various tracks were laid down before Led Zeppelin decided to continue work back at Headley Grange, using the Rolling Stones' mobile studio. Rehearsing the new material, the band sensed that everything was coming together. All of the album's backing tracks were completed at the Grange.

In February Led Zeppelin were back at Island Studios working on the overdubs. Sandy Denny (previously of Fairport Convention) duetted with Robert on 'The Battle of Evermore' while Jimmy laid down the solo for 'Stairway to Heaven' in one take. By the end of February all that remained was the final mix which was to be undertaken at Sunset Sound in Los Angeles, at the recommendation of engineer Andy Johns.

First there was the matter of the 'Return to the Clubs' tour, a month-long round of concerts at British universities and clubs that had first booked the young Led Zeppelin – and for the same fees. The first gig was at Belfast's Ulster Hall, where the band premiered two tracks from the new album, 'Black Dog' and 'Stairway to Heaven' with Jimmy playing his new custom-made double-necked Gibson guitar. The tour ended with a nostalgic visit to London's Marquee Club. Following the tour, BBC's Radio One broadcast an hour-long concert on 4 April, which included all the tracks from the new album.

It was time to mix the tracks of the new album, so Jimmy and Andy Johns headed to Los Angeles where they spent many weeks in the studio. The finished tape sounded great in L.A. but sounded terrible when played back in the studio in England. The result was a fast exit from Andy Johns and a frustrating delay while an engineer was found to remix the tracks. The new mix wasn't completed until the band returned from a planned European tour in July. That tour ended with a gig at Milan's Vigorelli stadium, which ended in a riot when the Italian police tried to keep 'order' by teargassing the audience. The band were forced to flee as the

audience rushed the stage to escape the batons of the riot police. In the melee that followed, Zeppelin's abandoned equipment was trashed.

Another metaphorical riot occurred when Atlantic Records were confronted with the sleeve artwork for the new album. There was no title and there was no mention of the band. The only clue was the credit to Jimmy Page as producer. Angered by the press hostility, Jimmy had decided that far from relying on 'hype' the band produced music that would sell itself. To add to the inscrutability of the cover, each band member was represented by a symbol (Plant by a feather in a circle, Jones by three ovals intersecting a circle, Bonham by three interlocking circles and Page by what looked like a bit like a Norse rune). The marketing men at Atlantic nearly had a collective nervous breakdown but the band was adamant – you don't get the master tapes until you agree to our cover. Knowing which side their bread was buttered, Atlantic backed down.

It was time to leave England's green and pleasant land for the mayhem and pleasures of touring. The seventh North American tour opened in Vancouver on 19 August and ended in Honolulu in mid-September. After a brief holiday in Hawaii, Led Zeppelin headed for a five date tour of Japan. Although in a new country, the group's outrageous behaviour continued. So much damage was done to the Tokyo Hilton that the group was banned for life. In October the band returned home, Jimmy and Robert taking a side trip to Thailand and India on the way back.

What was, in effect, *Led Zeppelin IV* was released in November. The critics liked it better than III, and the fans bought it, driving it quickly to number two in the US chart. In the UK, Zeppelin started a multi-city UK tour on 11 November, all concerts selling out in 24 hours. The high point of the tour was a two-night performance to 19,000 fans at the Empire Pool, Wembley. After a final gig in Salisbury on 15 December, the band took a break.

Group photo, 1970

Jimmy's solo appearance on the
Julie Felix show, April 1970

Julie Felix, Robert and Jimmy April 1970

Empire Pool,Wembley 1971

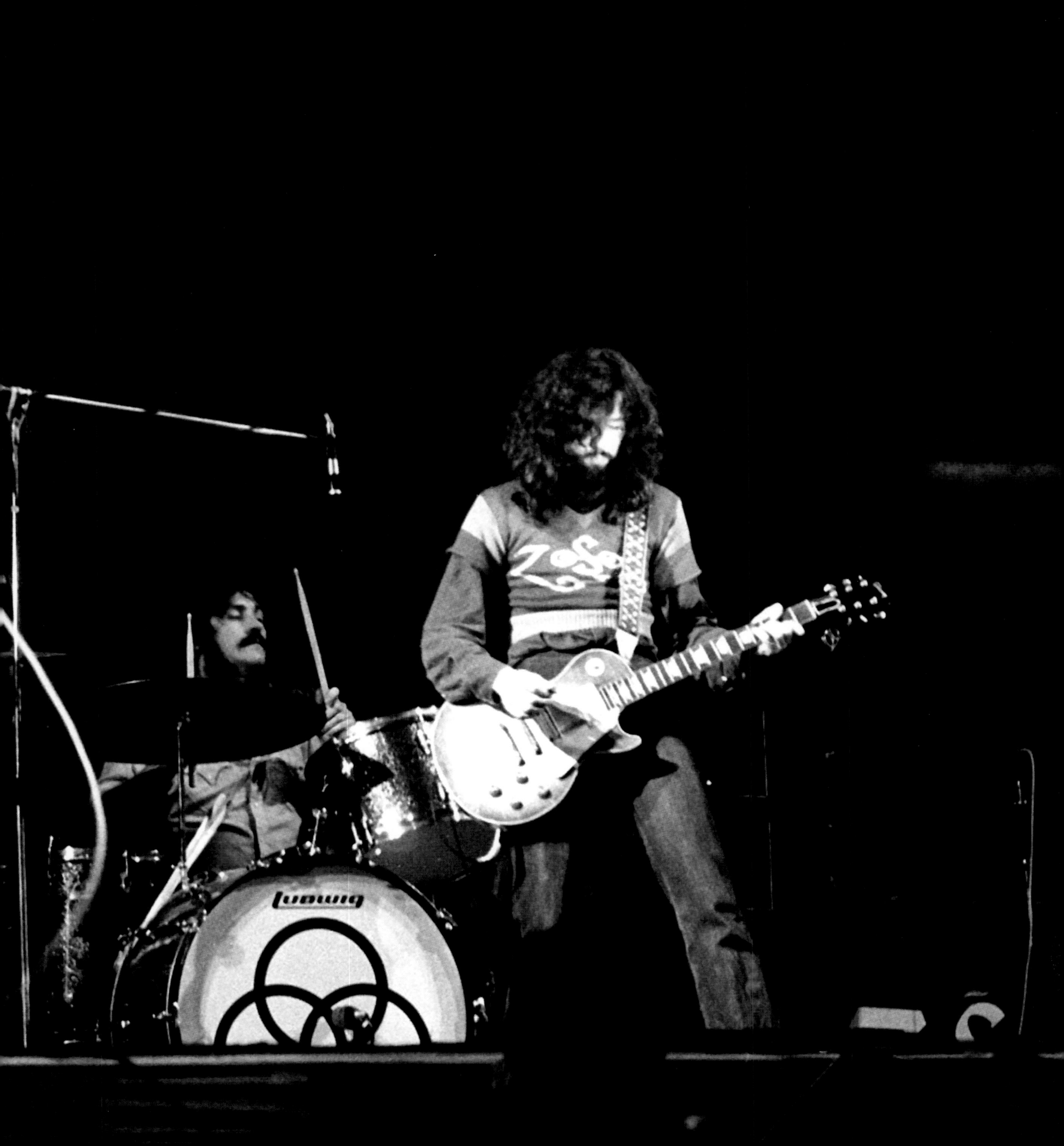

6. ON THE ROAD

In spite of their huge earnings, which enabled them to live like country gentlemen, Led Zeppelin needed the buzz they got from touring. In January 1972 they were rehearsing for their tour of Singapore, Australia and New Zealand and laying plans for their fifth album. Singapore never happened. They landed at Changi Airport the day before the concert, only to be refused entry because of their long hair. As they weren't even allowed to leave the plane they had to return to London. The first date of the tour became Perth, Australia on 16 February, followed by four more Australian gigs, a New Zealand performance and a massive closing show in Sydney on 10 March.

In April and May the group were back home recording tracks for their next album at Stargroves, a country house in Berkshire owned by Mick Jagger. Although the sessions were incredibly productive, once again a technical problem reared its head. The sound at Stargroves just wasn't 'right', leading to many months of studio time to correct the problem.

With the 1972 US tour looming, Peter Grant, the group's tough and astute manager, revolutionised the way that major rock groups were paid for touring. Rather than share the gate receipts fifty-fifty with the local promoter, Grant would act as the promoter, paying all the expenses. The local promoter would receive 10 percent of the gate for local organisation. Grant would hire the venues, carry the risk and take 90 percent of the gate for Led Zeppelin.

The risk, it appeared, was small. Most of the concerts in the summer North American tour were a sell-out without advertising. The tour was a financial and artistic success with the band on a performance high playing to huge audiences of ecstatic fans. The only problem was that the press largely ignored the tour, instead doting on the Rolling Stones, who were touring the US at the same time. To paraphrase Jimmy's acid comment – who wants to know about Led Zeppelin when Mick Jagger's hanging around with Truman Capote?

Nevertheless, the road still beckoned. In October Led Zeppelin were in Japan and then in Montreux for two dates at the end of the month. On 10 November the group announced a UK tour starting in December and ending in January 1973. In response the fans bought all 120,000 tickets in a day.

Sydney concert, Australian tour, 1972

Jimmy page on stage, Trentham
Gardens, Stoke on Trent, January 1973

European tour, 1973

7. LED ZEPPELIN FLIES

The December 1972 tour wound on into January 1973, finishing at the end of the month in Preston. The band spent February preparing for their March European tour and their May tour of the US. The European tour included gigs in Denmark, Norway, Sweden, Austria and Germany. On 26 March Led Zeppelin started a five-city tour of France, the same day as the new album *Houses of the Holy* was released. Even before the release, Zeppelin accounted for 18 per cent of Atlantic's sales. The percentage was to rise to nearer 30 per cent.

The American tour was to see many changes from previous years. A new stage rig was built and trialled at the Old Town Studios. It was decided that the hated press should be wooed and so an American press agent was hired. Peter Grant fired Led Zeppelin's New York booking agents, saving the group the ten percent commission. The tour was going to be enormous, visiting 33 cities, and was expected to gross $4.5 million. To accommodate Jimmy's fear of flying (except when drunk) and to streamline the tour arrangements Peter Grant chartered 'The Starship', a luxuriously converted Boeing 720B airliner.

As the group arrived in the US for their first show in Atlanta, *Houses of the Holy* reached number one in the American album charts. The first show attracted 49,000 fans, the second in Tampa, Florida, 56,000. 'The Starship' jetted the group around America, taking them to 18 more cities. Led Zeppelin had become like royalty. No busy airline terminals for them. Stretch limousines picked them up from the jet, parked discretely in the corner of the airfield, away from the milling crowds. The most satisfying headline of the tour came from the UK *Daily Express:* 'Believe it or not – they're bigger than the Beatles.'

Led Zeppelin's offstage behaviour was not regal. At their usual base, the Continental Hyatt House on Sunset Boulevard, Road Manager Richard Cole rode up and down the corridors on a motorcycle while furniture was heaved over the balconies - the TVs making a particularly satisfying explosive crunch as they landed. The first leg of the tour ended with a gig at the LA Forum on 3 June. There was a short holiday in Hawaii, then the band went their separate ways, to reconvene in Chicago for the first concert of the second leg of the tour on 6 July. In Baltimore Joe Massot, commissioned by Peter Grant, began shooting footage for a projected Led Zeppelin film. The crew were also in action in Pittsburgh, Boston and the last three shows at Madison Square Garden in New York. The group was checked into the prestigious Drake Hotel, exhausted at the end of a gruelling tour. Their fatigue showed in the lacklustre New York performances. During their stay at the hotel $203,000 belonging to the band was stolen from a safe deposit box, never to be seen again. Two days later the dazed and confused band members headed back across the Atlantic.

Back in the UK, the band members headed for their homes. In October, Joe Massot was at their homes as well, shooting everyday domestic activity as well as mini costume dramas representing each member of the band at vast expense. On a more serious level, Jimmy and the rest of the band were working on ideas for the next album at Headley Grange (suspended when John Paul Jones fell ill) while filmmaker Kenneth Anger was pressing Jimmy to complete the soundtrack of his movie *Lucifer Rising*. Perhaps still exhausted from the US tour, Jimmy felt a mixture of elation and anxiety, a clear view of his musical direction, but a sense of time closing in.

Performance at the Kezar Stadium, San Francisco, June 1973

Press conference on US tour, 1973

1973 US tour

THE YEAR THAT DIDN'T HAPPEN

8.

Led Zeppelin's original record deal with Atlantic expired at the end of 1973. In pursuit of their coveted freedom, the group decided to launch their own label, coupled to a distribution deal with Atlantic. The plan was not only to issue future Led Zeppelin albums on the label but also to actively search for new acts. The as-yet-to-be-named label opened an office on London's Kings Road.

Work on the sixth album re-started in January, again at Headley Grange. Fifteen tracks were laid down and mixed by mid-1974, but it would be some time before the double album was released. In the meantime, at least the label had a name. Various names had been floated, and rejected (Slag Records, Slut Records, Eclipse Records). Finally it was named Swan Song Records, after an acoustic guitar solo Jimmy had recorded. A new label, of course, needed launch parties. The first was a lunch held at the swanky Four Seasons restaurant in New York. Paul Rodgers, the lead singer from Swan Song signing Bad Company, enlivened the proceedings by throwing food at the head of Warner Communications, Atlantic's parent company.

The east coast taken care of, it was time to float the swan in Los Angeles. The group occupied their usual quarters on Sunset Strip, filling in the time before the party with their usual shenanigans involving a flock of infatuated young girls, various

members of the Led Zeppelin crew and a certain amount of intoxicating substances. The group emerged from their lair to meet Elvis Presley, who was appearing at the Los Angeles Forum. The audience lasted half an hour. Before they left Elvis asked for Led Zeppelin's autographs 'for my daughter Lisa-Marie'.

The party was held at the Bel Air Hotel. Of the movie stars invited only Groucho Marx and Lloyd Bridges bothered to show, together with the Stones' Bill Wyman and Roxy Music's Bryan Ferry. After the party the group went to the Rainbow Bar where Jimmy got into a row with a young female infatuee and, as so often in the past, road manager Richard Cole caused grievous bodily harm to a drunk who was causing the Zeppelin table some grief. Disconcertingly for the members of the group, a report of the party and the events at the Rainbow surfaced in the UK *Melody Maker* – they had told their wives that the party was in Denver.

The year rolled on. Bad Company's first album reached number one in the US album chart. Joe Massot was fired from the film project. Jimmy stole Ron Wood's wife. In October there was an outrageous party in Chiselhurst caves to launch the Pretty Things' album *Silk Torpedo*. The band hadn't played together in public for nearly 18 months. 1975 would be very different.

THOSE WHOM THE GODS WOULD DESTROY...

9.

At the beginning of 1975, Led Zeppelin left for what was planned to be a whole year on the road. They played warm-up dates in Brussels and Rotterdam, leaving for their tenth US tour in mid-January. The 40-show tour's 700,000 tickets sold out in 24 hours. The long-delayed double album *Physical Graffiti* was released on 24 February. With advance sales of $15 million, the album entered the US chart at number three, and soon climbed to number one. The excitement generated by the tour brought all the group's albums into the chart.

What a contrast with earlier tours. Not only was 'The Starship' rolled out again, the tour infrastructure of sound rigs, lights, dry ice machines required an army of roadies. It seemed that the band was at the zenith of its power but, from the beginning, there were bad omens. Jimmy had shut his left-hand ring finger in a train door just before the tour started. Robert developed flu, and four dates had to be cancelled. The shows just didn't seem to be coming together. There had always been lots of drugs but now heroin had joined the list. John Bonham was more and more out of control, performing brilliantly on stage but behaving more and more erratically offstage, fuelled by large amounts of alcohol. When the group arrived at the New York Plaza hotel, a $10,000 bond to cover possible damage was demanded. The first leg of the tour ended with a show at the Long Island Coliseum.

Exhausted, the band took a ten day break. Refreshed, Led Zeppelin launched into the second part of the tour. It went well enough but Jimmy, who had recently included the symbol 666 (the mark of the beast identified in the Book of Revelations) on his stage costumes, said 'I'd like to play for another 20 years... but I don't know, I just can't see it happening... It's just a funny feeling, a foreboding....'

In May the group performed a five night gig at London's Earl Court Arena. They were a triumph, with 20,000 fans each night worshiping at the shrine. After the show the band left the UK, the beginning of a year-long self-imposed exile for tax purposes. Robert and Jimmy went to Morocco, and then, after various adventures, drove across Spain and France to the band's tax exile base in Montreux. Reunited, the band began to plan new tours, including South America, and developed ideas of recording with Egyptian and Indian musicians.

Jimmy and Robert and their families took off to Rhodes for a summer holiday in July. On 3 August Jimmy left for Sicily (he was interested in buying a property formerly owned by Aleister Crowley, a mystic and occultist who fascinated him). The following day a rental car, driven by Maureen, Robert's wife, and containing Robert, their children and Jimmy's daughter Scarlett, skidded over a precipice and hit a tree. Scarlett was uninjured but Robert and the rest of his family were seriously hurt. They were flown home by air ambulance, but because of the tax avoidance scheme Robert had to recuperate in Jersey.

The touring plans for 1975 were in tatters, and with a consequent loss of earnings the group needed to look for alternative sources of income. A new album was bound to be a banker and they dusted off the footage of their projected film (they had already appointed a new director, Peter Clifton). They agreed to rendezvous in Los Angeles in September to start work on the album which was to be called *Presence.* Rehearsals finally got under way in October with Robert still in a wheelchair much of the time.

Once again, this time to avoid American tax, Led Zeppelin were on the move, recording and mixing *Presence* during three weeks in November at Musicland studios in Munich. Then it was back to Jersey, and an impromptu pub gig. The day before Christmas Robert, Bonzo and John Paul Jones headed to England and their families while workaholic Jimmy flew to New York to work on the soundtrack of the movie. Over Christmas Robert was able to walk without a walking stick for the first time since the accident.

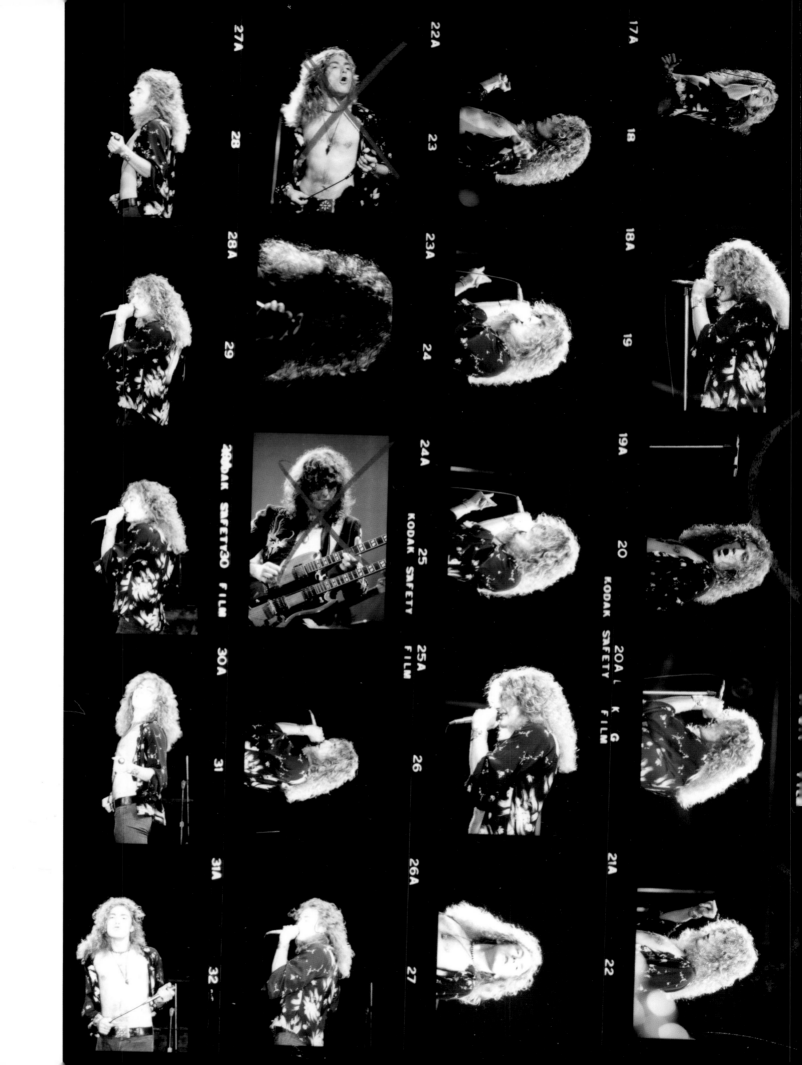

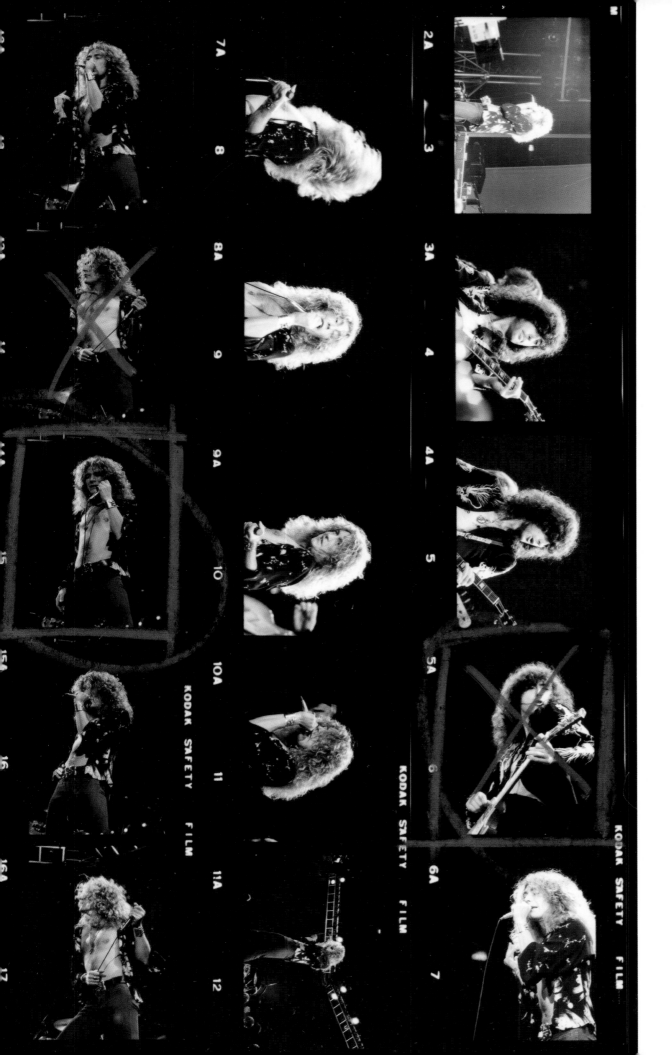

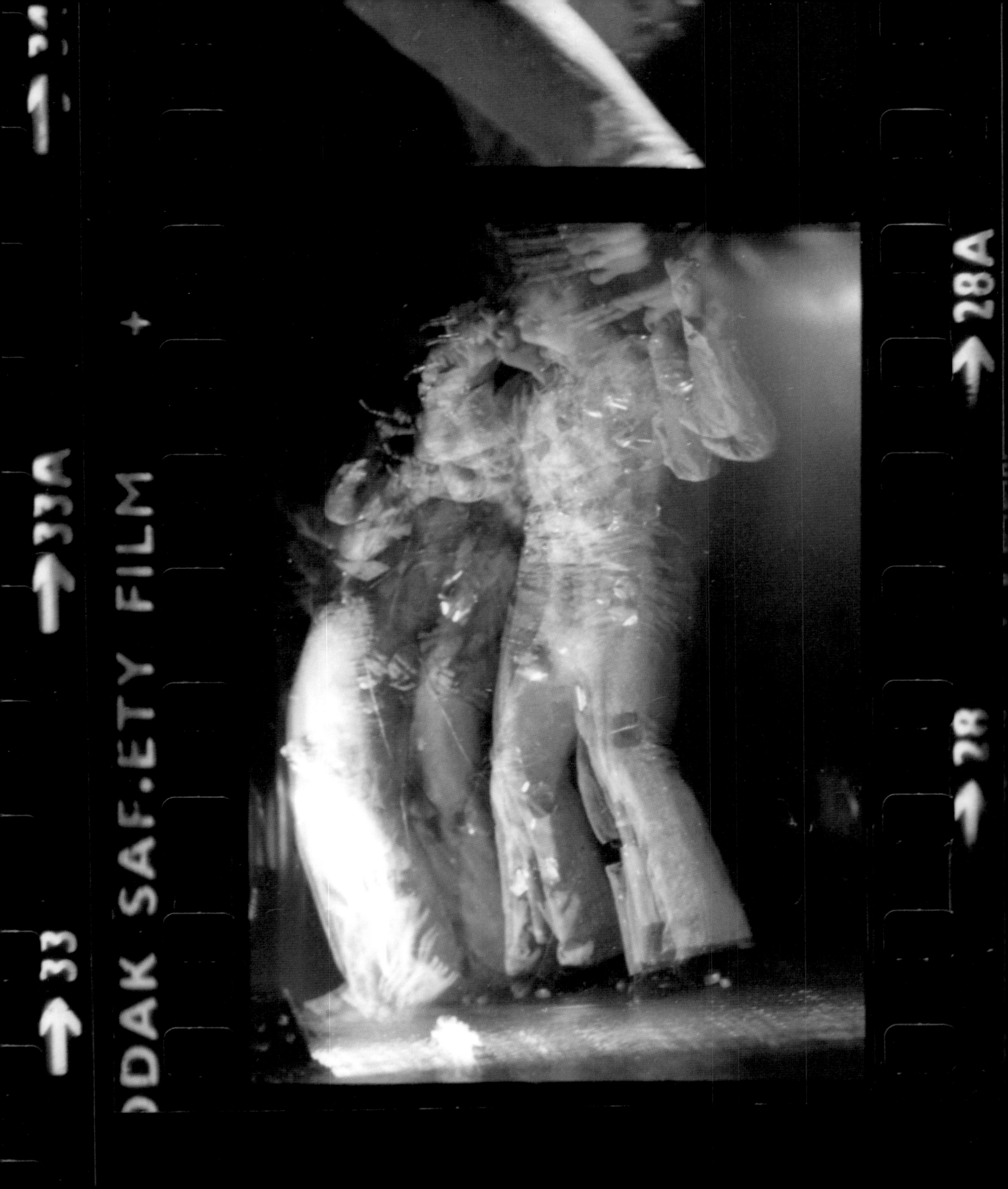

Earls Court, London, 1975

Earls Court, London, 1975

Earls Court, London, 1975

West Coast premier of *The Song Remains the Same*, 22 October 1976

10. DECLINE

Sometimes decline is closely preceded by what looks like triumph. After their Christmas break at home, the tax exiles were roughing it in New York's Park Lane Hotel, working on the soundtrack of the Led Zeppelin movie (now titled *The Song Remains the Same)* and the eponymous double soundtrack album. In February, Zeppelin won everything going in the *New Musical Express* reader's poll. In April *Presence* was released, achieving platinum status in the US with over one million advance orders. Robert and Jimmy joined Swan Song's big success Bad Company at several gigs.

On 20 October 1976 *The Song Remains the Same* was premiered in New York, followed by the release of the double album on 22 October, alongside the LA west coast premier. The European premier was to follow in London on 4 November. The soundtrack album went platinum but the film was only a modest success, described by the old enemy *Rolling Stone* as 'a tribute to their rapaciousness and inconsideration. While Led Zeppelin's music remains worthy of respect... their sense of themselves merits only contempt.' Even Jimmy admitted it was no masterpiece but a worthwhile tax write-off. The band had been off the road since May 1975 – nearly 18 months. In November and December they started rehearsing for what would be their eleventh tour of America in 1977.

With the tour scheduled to begin in March, the beginning of 1977 was spent in preparation. Sadly 'The Starship' was no longer available, so Peter Grant rented another flying gin palace from the owners of Las Vegas casino Caesar's Palace, modestly called 'Caesar's Chariot'. The beginning of the tour had to be postponed by a month because Robert had tonsillitis, finally kicking of on 1 April in Dallas, Texas. From a gig in Oklahoma City, Led Zeppelin moved on to a four-night engagement in Chicago. The performances now extended to over three hours, physically draining events for the band night after night. The first leg of the tour ended at the Pontiac Silverdome in Michigan, playing to a worshipping crowd of 76,000 on 30 April.

Taking a break, the whole band were at London's Grosvenor Hotel on 12 May to receive an Ivor Novello award for their 'outstanding contribution to British music'. Then it was back to the US for the second leg of the tour which started in Birmingham, Alabama. Following a cancelled gig in Tampa, Florida, it was on to New York and a sell-out six night residency at Madison Square Garden. Both Jimmy and Robert were at the top of their game. The west coast was next, with six triumphant nights at the LA forum.

After another break, the final leg got under way in Seattle, followed by two nights in San Francisco at the Oakland Coliseum on 23 and 24 July. On the first night a security man hired by Bill Graham, the promoter of the show, was badly beaten by Peter Grant and John Bindon, one of Led Zeppelin's security guards, while Richard Cole kept watch. Grant had been told that the man had been rough with his young son. The day after the second concert the Oakland police swooped and arrested Grant, Cole, Bindon and John Bonham. The four were charged with assault and released on $250 bail.

On 26 July, Led Zeppelin arrived in New Orleans in preparation for a concert on the 30th. On 27 July, in a phone call from his wife, Robert learnt that their son Karac had died as the result of a respiratory virus at the age of five. The tour was immediately abandoned and Robert flew back to England with John Bonham and Richard Cole.

With everything in suspense, inevitably there were rumours that the band would split, rumours strongly denied by the band. And so ended 1977.

US tour, 1977

US tour, 1977

US tour, 1977. John Paul Jones
playing his Andy Mason custom
triple neck guitar

Oakland Coliseum, 23 July 1977

Bonzo, Oakland Coliseum, 23 July 1977

Jimmy, Oakland Coliseum, 23 July 1977

Jimmy in the offices of Swansong
Records, 1977

118

Robert, John Paul Jones and Jimmy at London
radio station LBC August 1979.

11. ...AND FALL

Led Zeppelin was in limbo. Jimmy spent time listening to tapes of the group's live performances for a possible 'live' album. In February 1978 Bonham, Grant, Bindon and Cole were found guilty of the charges brought following the 1977 Oakland Coliseum fracas and were fined and given suspended sentences. Robert was with his family, incommunicado.

By April communication was re-established and Robert agreed to join the band for rehearsals. Led Zeppelin gathered at Clearwell Castle in the Forest of Dean to play together for the first time in months and to discuss the future. In the following months Robert began to sit in with various midlands bands and in August went to Ibiza to jam with Dr Feelgood. October arrived and found the band reunited as they began rehearsals for their next album. John Paul Jones had become the musical leader of the band and his themes and ideas matched with Robert's lyrics produced a more mature music. Rehearsals went well and the band was reinvigorated.

They left for Polar Studios in Stockholm at the beginning of December. The tracks for the album were completed in three weeks. Although the recorded music was very intense, the mood in the sessions was subdued.

Back home as 1979 dawned there were reasons to be cheerful. On January 21 Robert's wife Maureen gave birth to a baby boy. The band were elated with the music they had recorded in Stockholm – Jimmy, Robert and John returned to Sweden in February to mix the tracks of *In Through the Out Door.* In May came the news the fans had been waiting for – the band would play an outdoor show at Knebworth in Hertfordshire on 4 August, to coincide with the release of the new album. Such was the demand for tickets that another date on 11 August was announced. Not everything in the garden was rosy, with hostility from the music press and many of the new wave of punk bands.

Led Zeppelin hadn't played a show in the UK since 1975, and they wanted to make sure that they were ready to wow their fans. At the end of July they played two warm-up concerts in Copenhagen. On their return the band spent time refining the spectacular light show that would accompany their performances. The first show on 4 August went well enough, the second on 11 August was plagued with technical difficulties caused by rain. The reaction of the UK music press could be summed up by

the phrase 'dinosaur rock'. The fans were still loyal. In October the complete Led Zeppelin catalogue was in the *Billboard* Top 200 album chart, and there were enough loyal fans to earn the band seven awards in the *Melody Maker* readers' poll. So 1979 came and went.

The band were together again in April 1980, rehearsing for a 15-date European tour. On 17 June Led Zeppelin played the first show in Dortmund, followed by a series of dates in Germany, Holland, Belgium and Austria. This tour was different from the royal progresses of the past. Richard Cole, their road manager through so many campaigns, had been fired by Peter Grant and had ended up in an Italian prison. The lightshows and other special effects were slimmed down. Much of the time the band seemed exhausted. The Nuremburg concert had to be ended after three numbers when John Bonham collapsed. Nevertheless, Zeppelin made it to the end of the tour on 7 July.

On 11 September Peter Grant announced details of 'Led Zeppelin: The Eighties Part One' – a 19-date tour starting at the Montreal Forum on 17 October. On 24 September Bonham was driven to Bray Studios in Berkshire to meet up with the other members of the band for the first rehearsal in preparation for the tour. He started drinking en route and continued drinking during the rehearsal and afterwards at a band party at Jimmy's new house in Windsor. Bonham passed out on a sofa and was carried to a bedroom to sleep it off. Around 1.45 pm the following day a member of Jimmy's staff went to wake him – and was shocked to discover that Bonzo was dead.

An inquest determined that John Bonham had died from an overdose of alcohol, having consumed 40 measures of vodka and then having choked on his own vomit. He was buried at Rushock parish church near his home on 10 October 1980. He was 31 years old and he left behind his wife Pat and children Jason and Zoe.

The surviving members of Led Zeppelin issued this statement on 4 December. 'We wish it to be known that the loss of our dear friend, and the deep respect we have for his family, together with the deep sense of harmony felt by ourselves and our manager, have led us to decided that we could not continue as we were.'

Forest National Stadium, Belgium,
European tour, 1980

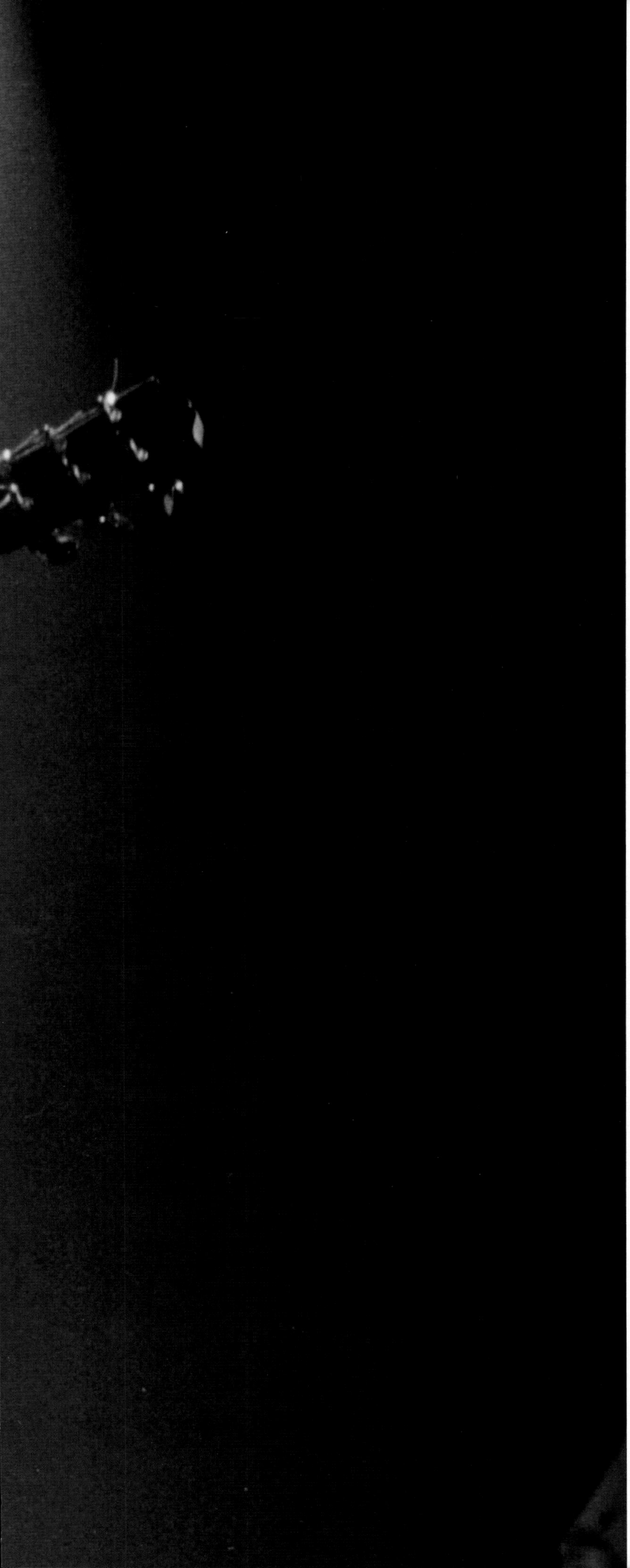

The Firm

John Bonham's gravestone,
Rushock, Worcestershire.

12. AFTERMATH

Without the anchor of Led Zeppelin, the remaining members drifted apart. John Paul Jones made the most decisive break as that persona was largely retired and John Baldwin re-emerged to return to his family and his farm. Eventually he was to emerge on the other side of the studio glass as a producer. Jimmy worked on the score for *Death Wish II*. Robert started to develop a new musical style and in June 1982 released his first solo album *Pictures at Eleven*. Heavily influenced by Arabic music, the album reached number three in the US chart and number two in the UK. The final Led Zeppelin album, *Coda*, was issued in December 1982, containing eight out-takes from sessions dating back as far as *Led Zeppelin II*. The album entered the US chart at number four and sold respectably for the rest of the year.

Both Jimmy and Robert did some touring, Robert as a solo act, Jimmy in a charity fund-raising tour for ARMS (Action into Multiple Sclerosis), and then with 'The Firm'. In 1984 Robert and Jimmy worked in a studio together for the first time since they had rehearsed just before Bonham's death. The EP of classic rock songs, released on Robert's label Es Paranza (Robert had quit Swan Song some time ago) reached number four in the American charts.

In July 1985 the three remaining members of the group (with Phil Collins on drums) played three numbers at the Live Aid show in Philadelphia and got a tumultuous reception, and in May 1988 the group, with Bonham's son Jason on drums, played a set at the fortieth anniversary of Atlantic records. In 1995 Jimmy, Robert and John Paul Jones were at New York's Waldorf-Astoria to be inducted into the Rock & Roll Hall of Fame. They played a set with the two lead members of Aerosmith, and then a finale – 'When the Levee Breaks' – with Neil Young and Michael Lee. In 1998, Page and Plant appeared together at the Reading Festival.

In 1990 Jimmy remastered the band's catalogue for release on the 1990 box set *Led Zeppelin* which became the biggest-selling box set of all time. This was followed three years later by the ten-disc set *Complete Studio Recordings* and in 2003 there was a three disc set of material recorded live during the 1972 tour of southern California and a Led Zeppelin DVD – more than five hours of taped interviews, TV shows and live performance. 'Stairway to Heaven' remains the most requested and most played song on FM radio in the USA. In a 2007 poll by UK radio company Smooth Radio 'Stairway to Heaven' was number two and 'Whole Lotta Love' number ten in a listeners' poll of 'Top 10 Songs for Over-50s'.

On 10 December 2007 Led Zeppelin, with Jason Bonham replacing his late father on drums, played their first full concert since 1980 in front of an audience of 22,000 at London's O2 Arena. This one-off show was dedicated to Ahmet Ertegun, the co-founder of Atlantic Records who had signed Led Zeppelin in 1968 (Ertegun had died in 2006). The proceeds of the concert went to the Ahmet Ertegun Education Fund. The band's performance received universal praise. The *New Musical Express* summed it up – 'What they have done here tonight is proof that they can still perform to the level that originally earned them their legendary reputation... We can only hope this isn't the last we see of them'.

Nordhoff Robbins Music Therapy concert,
Knebworth, June 1990

Robert Plant with Roger Taylor and
Brian May, Freddie Mercury tribute
concert, Wembley, April 1992

Page and Plant, Reading, 1998

Following the end of the Swansong label in 1983 Peter Grant virtually retired to his home in Eastbourne on the south coast of England where respectability overtook him. He was even offered (but turned down) the opportunity to become a magistrate. He died of a hear attack in November 1995 at the age of 60. His funeral was held on 4 December – the 15th anniversary of Led Zeppelin's break-up.

Robert Plant, Pete Townsend and
Roger Daltrey, Hyde Park, 1996

ARMS concert, Jimmy Page and Eric Clapton

Robert, John Paul Jones and Jimmy at
a screening of the 'Led Zeppelin DVD'
May 2003.

In 2003 'School of Rock' star Jack Black convinced Led Zeppelin (notoriously reluctant to grant permission for the use of their music) to allow the use of 'Immigrant Song' in the movie by recording a specially videotaped plea to the band on the film set.

Jimmy with his MBE,
14 December 2005.
It was awarded for
Jimmy's work with
street children in Brazil

Jimmy at the UK Music Hall of Fame, Alexandra Palace, London, November 2006

INDEX

PHOTOGRAPHER CREDITS